# Golf

## made easier...
## not easy

Rocky —
I didn't forget
you. Thanks,

Bruce Fossum

Oct 2, 1992

Golfish, Inc., in cooperation with Medi-Ed Press
Post Office Box 545, Okemos, MI 48805

© 1989 Golfish, Inc.

Printed in the USA by BookCrafters, Inc., Chelsea, Michigan.

Cover design and illustrations by Mary Ann Kiesler, Art by Design,
    1977 Riveria Drive, East Lansing, Michigan 48823.

Book production by Medi-Ed Press, 9353 Honeywood Ct., Orange-
    vale, California 95662.

**Library of Congress Cataloging-in-Publication Data**

Fossum, Bruce.
        Golf made easier. . . not easy.
        "Published in cooperation with Medi-Ed Press."
        1. Golf.  I. Title.
GV965.F634  1989          796.352'3          88-31577
ISBN  0-936741-03-1

# Golf

## made easier...
## not easy

**by Bruce Fossum**

# Contents

# Foreword by Jud Heathcote

Why am I, a longtime coach of a team sport, writing the foreword for a golf book? I guess it's because, like you, I am an avid golf enthusiast. In golf there is no team to beat. You may compete against an opponent, but you are really competing against the course and yourself.

Regardless of our golfing ability, we all strive for improvement. Reading this book *will* improve your golf game. Studying this book will improve it even more.

Coach Fossum has done a masterful job of assimilating a tremendous amount of information in an easy-to-read, easy-to-understand manner. Bruce, through years of teaching and coaching experience, has captured on paper the helpful hints and teaching principles that have not only made him a great coach and teacher, but have put him in the Golf Coaches Hall of Fame. He has stressed the mental, as well as the physical, approach to playing and enjoying the game of golf.

This book will improve your swing, your shot, and *your score.*

# About the Author

Bruce Fossum loves to play golf and, like anyone who has ever teed it up, knows just how satisfying—and frustrating—the sport can be.

An Associate Professor in the Health and Physical Education Department, "Coach" is a nationally known administrator, teacher, writer and coach of golf. He has had a winning golf program at Michigan State University for 24 years. He chaired the NCAA Golf Committee from 1972 to 1975 and presided over the Golf Coaches Association of America from 1977 to 1979. Three years ago, he was inducted into the Golf Coach's Hall of Fame for his fine contribution to college golf.

As a professional, he has dealt with thousands of people through clinics, workshops, private lessons, and the university. Bruce has been a clinician for the Lifetime Sports Education Project and the National Golf Foundation. He is co-author of an award winning book entitled Golf.

His wife, Mary, is the women's golf coach at Michigan State and his son, Bob, captained the MSU golf team in 1984 and 1985. In addition to playing golf, "Coach" also enjoys fly fishing the rivers of Michigan whenever he gets the chance.

# Introduction

*Golf made easier—not easy* was conceived while I was working on a series of golf articles for the Lansing (Michigan) State Journal in the winter of 1987. It is intended for the avid golfer, and that happens to be you.

Many of us don't have the time to practice much. Some of us simply would rather just play the game than spend time on the practice tee. This book will help you play more effectively by using your personal talents better than you now do. It will teach you ways to play that don't demand a lot of practice, though I urge you to do so whenever you can. You will learn to use shots—that you already know how to make—in the right places.

The book shows you how to play "smart" golf as well as adding some new weapons to your arsenal. This all helps to lower your scores as well as make golf more interesting and exciting to play.

You won't find any pictures or illustrations in this book to either help or confuse you. It is meant for pleasurable reading and thoughtfulness. You will find that you can pick it up and read all or any part of it for your enjoyment.

I think that you, as an avid and interested golf player, will find many helpful points in this book and will really appreciate golf all the more for reading it.

Bruce Fossum

# Acknowledgments

Thanks to Mary Ann Kiesler of Art by Design, East Lansing, Michigan, who designed the cover and did the art work for this book. She is a very talented graphic artist and a true professional in this industry. Michigan State University has been fortunate to have her on staff for 26 years.

Jud Heathcote, the basketball coach at Michigan State University, was the winner in the contest to name this book. Consequently, he was coerced into writing the Foreword. He is an avid golfer and a true competitor. Thanks to Jud for his usual adroitness and, of course, for his winning title.

Terry Fossum, #1 daughter, proofread the manuscript for me in its various stages of preparation; thank goodness and thank you, Terry.

Sherlyn Martens put all of this together in book form and did a nice job of guiding it through the book production process.

# 1 Opening Shot

What is it that we all seek to accomplish in this most difficult game of golf? What intrigues us? What makes us keep coming back, in a lot of cases, for more punishment? What can turn a smiling pussycat into a raving maniac all in one swing of a club? Or vice versa? It is not usually the score, my avid player; it's *the shot!* We either love it or hate it. It's the shot we remember.

How about that chip shot that Larry Mize made to win the 1987 Masters? How could one forget? Now, what was his score that put him in that famous play-off?

Hard to remember, isn't it?

Think of one of your great shots from last summer. Perhaps it was the drive which carried the top of the hill on that tough #14, a thing of beauty. Or maybe the putt on #11, that little gem of 40 feet that took three breaks before it fell in the side of the cup for your first birdie ever on that hole.

We remember those. I, like you, try to forget the bad ones. But it's hard. I hit so many. If I could just make those bad ones *not so bad*.

THE SHOT. That's what this game is all about.

The PGA Tour player hits a whole bunch of good shots, hopefully makes a lot of money, and maybe steals a tournament win if the putter works just right. The average high handicapper hits very few good shots, but when he does he is very proud and happy.

Regardless of your skill, you are either elated or dejected with your shot results. Thrilled by the best; more determined by the worst.

Making the good shot is fun. It's that simple. You don't whisper about the good shot, you tell the whole world. That's a big reason why I play golf. I'm guessing that's why you do too. It's fun to win some battles along the way—even if you don't always win the war.

# 2 Happy Shots Help You to Score

The score you make in a given round of golf is nothing but a reflection on how many good or bad shots you hit. If your score is good, you announce it proudly. If it's not up to your standards, you might say you hit some really good shots but it didn't show up on the card.

So right now, let's define just what a good shot is. I say a good shot is one that gets from point A to point B. It's that simple. Lots of shots are good-looking. But many end in disaster due to either a slight physical malfunction or bad thinking.

Scoring is the result of the accumulation of shots. Each one is important. And it's quite obvious that there is a nice hook-up between low scores and good shots.

But you don't have to be Lee Trevino to make good golf shots. Just remember these two things:

○ **Take a good look at your strengths in golf and stick with them.**

○ **Give each shot proper thought before pulling a club out of the bag.**

To reinforce these two items, if you have any doubt whatsoever about hitting a certain kind of shot— DON'T!!

If you want to score better and hit better shots, take hold of your vanity, assess your talents, and hit nice shots that will play well and make you happy. Usually these 'happy' shots are played from "the short grass." It's tough to play from behind trees and shrubs, from deep grass, or from the depths of a creek or pond.

Never make an uncertain play or hit an uncertain shot unless it's just for the heck of it.

If I ever made even close to an *absolute* comment about golf, this would be it: "You can have a heckuva swing and know how to play the game, but if you don't play a lot, you have to lower your scoring sights somewhat." And that's hard if you're a competitor; it's difficult to accept higher numbers than you know you are capable of making.

When you can't play a lot, I would suggest that if you want to develop your skills to the fullest extent, use your time to practice the good stuff, then try to think well on the course. Golf, being the teeter-totter game it usually is, will probably be more forgiving to you for doing this and your scores will be more consistently low.

# 3 Getting into the Swing of Things

No, not another swing lesson. There are good teachers to be found to help you with that. Books and videos are plentiful and full of information backed by history and scientific facts. But I can only associate good swings with good shots. That's what I would like to convey.

I honestly don't know what a good swing is. Results seem to justify what the player is doing with the swing. I have observed many swings, and the only absolute in each of them is that they are all different.

There is one constant in swings of great players. They appear to be in good balance throughout the swing. This is testimony to their set-up which allows them to hold steadier than the average bear as they get into motion without rushing things.

Try to develop a productive swing—one you can understand so you can make minor adjustments to it when the ball is going crooked. Get a swing that you can trust in tense situations.

It's fun to be able to face a shot, step up and swing the club without thinking of a dozen things. Players who constantly review aspects of their swing have developed that well-known disease, *Paralysis through Analysis.* These players should seek help in isolating their thoughts. Good players have only one swing thought—if that.

Never play a careless shot. Think out the possibilities in a positive way. Make a decision on a club and shot. Know what to do prior to stepping up to the ball. Then try hard to execute. We are all guilty of neglect here. Get in better position by thinking each shot out.

We all need to work on these next two items. Improvement in each of these points will enable us to make better scores:

○ **Practice the short game.** At least 60 percent of the game is made up of pitching, chipping and putting. Improving these shots is the easiest way to lower your scores. Your back yard or living room can be used as your laboratory.

○ **Learn to accept each shot for what it is, then go on to the next one.** This is the most difficult lesson to learn. The last shot is history. Concentrate on the present shot. Many games have been destroyed by the inability of the player to maintain emotional control following a bad shot. Every player should be able to accept credit for a good shot, and accept blame for a bad shot.

Some improvement is possible by playing a lot of golf. But it will be limited. To improve, changes—adjustments—must be made. Serious golfers should seek professional advice and be prepared to set time aside for practice.

Players who don't or can't take lessons from a professional—or fail to set time aside for practice—must accept the inevitable results, and learn to live in their 'comfort zone.'

## PRACTICE TIPS

○ **Plan your practice for improvement and fun.** Haphazard ball-hitting can often do as much harm as good.

○ **Practice your best shots.**

○ **Always play to or aim at a specific target.**

○ **Lay a club or a similar item on the ground and point it toward the target to guide your alignment.** Place this between your feet and the ball.

○ **Take your time between shots**. Observe ball flight.

○ **Low handicap players should work on weaknesses or new shots.**

○ **Practice in an area where the distance of each shot can be determined.** Know how far a good shot with each club will fly in the air.

# 4 Quickness Can Ruin Your Game

Picture yourself on the first tee at your local course. You're about to hit your first shot of the day.

All the eyes in the area are focused on you. At least, that's what you usually feel, isn't it? Do you get a yearning to want to get it over with?

If you're nervous, you're very normal. All of a sudden, anxieties have set in, creating muscle tension and indecision, thus making swinging a golf club that much more difficult.

Visualize the nice swing we usually apply while warming up for a round or while practicing. It becomes quite a puzzle when that very swing disappears once the game begins.

That beautiful rhythm we felt before the round suddenly becomes spastic and we begin to hit at the ball instead of swinging the club. We begin to search and try to find the swing we lost. What started as a nice day on the practice range begins to turn into a nightmare of frustration.

What happened?

In a physical sense, the anxieties mentioned above have created muscle tightness and have quickened our body movements. Motion becomes restricted and, of course, that beautiful rhythm we felt earlier is lost. Mentally we are affected by the fact that now every swing we take really counts. *We begin to deal in results rather than in preparation for the next shot.* We begin to deal in numbers instead of performance. We're in trouble!

Do the following thoughts sound familiar? "I just bogeyed the first three holes. Now I have to make some birdies to catch up." "I'm going to lose all my bets." "My score has to be posted on the scoreboard." "I'm really embarrassed about the way I'm playing." "I can't do anything right today." "All my friends will see my scores in the paper."

These anxieties, whatever they may be, create the question most asked of me, "What is the most common fault in golf?"

My pat answer—"Doing something too quickly." This "something" could be a physical move or possibly a mental decision. Starting the backswing too quickly with a herky-jerky move is the most common physical error. It is followed closely by its counterpart, starting the downswing too quickly in the transition period.

Mental errors are made too quickly due to either lack of knowledge, vanity, or perhaps too much familiarity with a given golf course or shot. Example: "I always hit a four-iron on this hole."

We can't be blamed for wanting to perform or score well. Good shots and good scores are what we really strive for. So, what can we do when we get anxious and really try too hard? How can we let our nice swing make good shots that might lead to better scores?

Here are my hints to you:

○ **The most obvious is to practice your swing enough so you have confidence in it and can trust it when all eyes are upon you.** As we have already concluded, this is quite difficult for many of us.

○ **Develop a specific pre-shot routine for every shot.** Beyond good hard practice, this idea of shot preparation is, in my mind, the most important thing you can do to relieve tension. Develop a regular routine before every shot. Doing this keeps the mind busy and away from preoccupation, distractions and results.

○ **This routine could begin in back of the ball where you can envision the shot in a positive manner (see the ball fly).** This gets you started nicely into your routine of grip, posture, and aiming at your target.

○ **Practice deep breathing in moments of tension.** Walk away from the shot, take a couple of deep breaths, then resume your performance. Top players sometimes work on relaxation training methods that they use when under extreme pressure. These methods are available, can be studied, and should be practiced before trying to use them in competition.

○ **Finally, if you are competing, try to keep your total daily routine in a sense of normality.** Keep things familiar. No surprises.

If you practice these things, you shouldn't be surprised when your shots and scores improve.

# 5 The Enigma of Ball Flight

One of the truly fascinating studies in golf and probably an enigma to most of us is the variety of crazy flight patterns a ball decides to take more frequently than we would like.

To me, these flights are a clue to the kind of swing the player made. Most players wonder what happened. The ball just sits there. It responds to being struck by the face of the club. It goes where the clubface sends it.

My hobby is fly-fishing. One day I was fishing on a stream that bordered along the edge of a golf course. A golf ball came slicing and humming by me and splashed to a watery grave right where I was casting. I began fishing once again when a young man came over in search of his ball. As I told him of the ball's fate, I hooked into a nice trout and my onlooker watched me play and land the fish. He asked me how I caught such a nice fish. I responded, "I thought like a trout." He walked away mumbling something to himself that sounded like, "Maybe if I thought like a golf ball?"

The story is a bit facetious, but perhaps it will set the tempo for what we have to say about ball flight.

The ball goes where the clubface makes it go. You swing the club and the clubhead hits the ball. The following things must happen to get good shot results: The clubhead must be traveling toward the target on line; it must have the correct speed for the shot; it must have a square face; and it must have the correct angle of attack to get the ball airborne, or rolling well, as the case might be. These factors: speed, path, face, and angle of attack are measured at the moment of impact—clubface on ball.

Now, let me give you some of the fundamentals that influence these all-important factors and one example of a negative result for each one.

Clubhead speed can be improved in quite a few ways. Increased use of the wrist lever and better timing are possibilities. When you swing full at the ball with any club and the shot is very low and shorter than you would like, you need more speed.

A good path of the clubhead down the target line at impact is controlled by a good armswing and shoulder-turn into the backswing as you hold center. Picking the club up with the hands and arms changes this path from outside to inside and causes hitting to the left and also aids a slice.

The face of the club is controlled largely by the grip. Make sure you have a workable grip for you; try to get the club into a fairly square position at the top of the swing. Inconsistent flight patterns usually indicate a grip that is suspect. Some experimentation should be done to find the best ball flight.

A good angle of attack can be promoted with good ball position and proper weight transfer plus that all-important center holding steady. Repeated pop-ups, topped shots, or those low snake-killers call for an overhaul of this important factor.

Now that we have an idea of what really happens to our golf ball, let's take a quick look at a very positive approach in developing good fundamentals in a swing.

○ **Learn a good grip that is soft but in control.** A lot of us hold too tightly and freeze our forearms, especially our dominant forearm. Develop good posture so you can swing the club in balance. Always align to the target.

○ **Learn to let your weight flow back on the inside of the right foot into the backswing and then back onto the left foot in the downswing.**

○ **Practice holding your head steady throughout the swing.** This simulates a center for your shoulders to turn around and your arms to swing around. It promotes balance and stability in the lower body and all of this improves both distance and direction.

○ **Work on a good release of the hands through the ball.** This will promote distance and square the face up for better direction. If you have finished your swing and the right hand has turned over the top of the left, you have released the clubhead.

How well you do the above depends on your mentor, if you have one, and, of course, your own feelings and efforts.

# 6 Need More Distance?

Few things in life are as discouraging to an avid golfer as a wimpy drive. After all, a big part of the fun of golf is ripping that good tee shot.

Most men like to swing hard and hit far—even at the expense of direction. Most women would lower their score a ton if they could learn to hit the ball farther. Senior players would give half their retirement check to hit it another 30 yards.

The question most asked of me in this regard is, "How far must a player hit the ball to be good today?" My pat answer is this: "Far enough."

Distance is relative to the class of competition, the player's skill, and the need for it.

I guess what you would like to know, however, is how can you hit it farther.

There are a lot of ways to get it done. Here are a few thoughts for you to consider.

*Learn to use your lever system correctly.* My teaching experience has shown me that the one fundamental missing in most of my students, young and old, is either the failure to cock the wrists properly into the backswing or the uncocking (releasing) of the same lever in the through-swing.

Setting this wrist angle properly can be learned, again, with good help.

When you get to the top of your backswing, the back of your left hand should be on the same plane as the back of your wrist and you should see some wrinkles at the base of the left thumb (if you are righthanded). This is called a "flat" wrist. *Get a club out and try some of this.*

It takes some doing to consistently get into this position. Swinging with your elbows close together helps considerably. Assuming you started with a good grip for you, the club will now be in a square position as you prepare to start the downswing.

A lot of guys get their left wrist into a cupped position (left wrist bending back when you reach the height of the backswing) with the wrinkles showing on the back of the hand and wrist. A little bit of this isn't bad, but a lot of it indicates an open clubface and usually results in the dreaded slice. Another way to tell that it is wide open is when the toe of the club is pointing straight down at the ground. What happens is that if you play with an open clubface at the top of your swing, you must find a way to square it up coming back down and through the shot or concede to the slice. Really what happens here is that you put the club into your hands and create a hitting action which leads to inconsistency. By learning a good wrist position, it is much easier to *swing* your arms—and the club. You will find the ball will go closer to where you want it to go and be hit much harder for the same, or less, effort.

Many players "lay the club off" (allow the left wrist to bend forward) at the top of the swing. This leads to a closed clubface and those low-left shots that don't go very far.

Once you get into the correct position, you have a good chance to hit the ball hard and straight.

A lot of players release the wrists too soon and cause a "casting" of the club on the downswing. That's fine for fishing, not for golf. The key to good timing of the hit, or release, *is to keep the right-hand grip as passive as possible when starting the transition into the downswing,* letting the left-hand grip trigger the action. This transition period, though brief, is so very vital. Usually this is where and when most of us get too quick, especially when the pressure is on. Practice a nice, easy start into the downswing and you will be able to naturally accelerate the clubhead through the ball instead of before the ball. Early release, or casting, leads to high and weak shots. We can do without those. Let's nail it!!

Many people with good timing will uncock their wrists AT THE BALL, but this still leaves the clubface slightly open and the ball will go to the right. If this is what you do, learn to make the right hand turn over and get on top of the left as you swing THROUGH THE BALL. This squares the clubface; in addition, it increases the speed of the clubhead and gives you more power!!

*Secondly, get the legs and lower body into the act.* Many of us waste this opportunity right off the bat by setting up with our weight too much up on the balls of our feet. Set your weight more to the heels and get a comfortable feel through the legs. Kind of bounce up and down in this position and feel the strength and balance that you feel in the whole upper body. Give it a try!

*There's a lot of exciting and sometimes very exotic equipment offered on the market today.* Modern technology has given us balls that go further, shafts that give the clubhead more speed, iron heads that forgive bad hits, and all types of wood?? heads that help increase distance. Who knows, modern technology might provide you with the right combination of ball, shaft, and head to help give you the length you are seeking.

*You could play with longer clubs.* This increases the width of your arc (radius of your swing) and, with just a little work on the timing, you could learn to use them to hit farther.

*Finally, you might want to work on developing more centrifugal force in your swing by learning to hold center better as you swing.* Good players concentrate on this at all times, but especially when they want to hit hard or when they have to face up to a particularly difficult shot.

Hitting hard and far is fun. As you try different methods to increase your chances, remember that your best scores are made when you play on the short grass. When you hit far and crooked, you may be living in the fast lane of power, but you will have to learn to cope with the penalties and/or recovery shots, as the case may be.

How far should you hit it? Far enough.

# 7 Putting Magic

Putting a golf ball is really a simple task when you stop and think about it—to stroke a ball just hard enough to get it rolling across a few feet of real estate.

I know it's frustrating, especially the close misses—and particularly those we leave short by inches. It often seems cruel when we lip one out and even inhuman when a putt doesn't take that last break we had read into it.

Nevertheless, putting is the most important part of the game and if you're interested in improving your scores it would behoove you to find ways to do it better.

Putting is approximately 40 percent of the Tour player's game and I suspect about 30 to 35 percent of yours. That to me is top priority stuff.

It can be easy! Work on a good stroke and don't worry about it so much! Do your homework by reading the putt and then make a good stroke. If you can learn to make your little putts with some consistency and once in a while pop a big one—that's good.

Beyond four or five feet, I feel lucky and very happy when I make one. Lucky because it *is* luck when the ball rolls over all the funny little things on the green; happy because I did my homework.

Here are some hints to help your putting:

○ **Like all shots, the two important shot results are distance and direction.** Of the two, distance is much more important!! Be sure to work some on uphill and downhill putts for distance feel as well as the level putts you get on most practice greens.

○ **Practice your putting stroke between a pair of two-by-fours to develop a good path and a square face.** You get good feedback if the putter touches the boards.

○ **Do not move your head during the putting stroke.**

○ **From the waist down, be positively still during the stroke.**

○ **Develop a pre-putt routine and do it every time, whether a 60-footer or a 6-inch.** This is the same as a pre-shot routine and for the same reasons—to rid yourself of anxieties.

○ **When setting up, line the putter up to**

the proposed line and then think distance.

○ **Begin reading your putt as you approach the green from the front.** Usually you can see the general tendencies of the slopes involved. Specifically, read the putt from a low position about 15 to 20 feet behind the ball looking toward the hole. Your first look is the best one in determining line.

○ **On long putts or putts that break a lot, it is much better to lag the ball to the hole. Learn to two-putt!!** This could be the most vital lesson of all!

○ **Be positive enough to think it is possible to make every putt, but be realistic enough to know what the odds are.**

○ **You might check into a grip change.** I recommend the reverse overlap grip in one of its variations.

○ **The most common error in the putting stroke is to allow the left wrist to break down at contact.** Keep the back of the left hand moving toward the target.

○ **In regard to putters: if you develop a good stroke, you can putt with a sledge hammer.** Problems are generally with the puttee, not the putter. Get one that feels and looks good to you and give it a chance.

Here are my favorite putting drills:

○ **Putt at a small target such as a tee stuck in the turf.**

○ **Place four balls on the compass points approximately one foot from the hole. Concentrate and make each one.** If you miss one, repeat the drill until you make each one. Then move the balls to two feet and repeat, then to three feet, etc.

○ **Putt 20 three-footers until you make them all.** The sight and sound of making putts builds confidence.

○ **Putt long putts to feel for distance.** Place tees or balls a foot on each side of the hole to enlarge the target. (When playing, I recommend that you have the flagstick attended when putting long putts. You will get a good perspective and feel for both distance and direction.)

# 8 Respectful Preparation for the Game

A personal gratification for me is to watch my players and students play smart golf, to watch their mental development as the game helps them grow up.

They not only learn to play better through practice and change, but they learn how to REALLY PLAY THE GAME! They develop a feel for scoring through countless experiences of success and failure. They learn how to use their talents on each shot.

They learn to attack when in position and are willing to accept the challenge of a difficult shot. They recognize when to back off when the conditions warrant, sometimes even "paying the golf course back" to escape a big number. They study the short shots with diligence and try to figure out how to get the ball close to the hole.

They grow in the game and are constantly challenged by its difficulty. And as they lose most of the wars but win a few battles along the way, I see a healthy, respectful attitude develop. I see determination in their eyes.

In the following chapters we're going to take a look at this mental side of golf. Earlier, I said if you made nice shots and thought about each one in preparation, you could improve your scores, regardless of your ball-striking ability. Try now to take your talents and apply some of the following to see if there might be some improvement on the bottom line.

Let's look at some of the things that you can do before you even strike the first ball:

○ **Find out how far you can hit the ball with each club in your bag—in the air!** If you are a high handicapper, find out, at least in approximation, how far you can expect to have the ball go with a decent shot using any club. Don't forget that golf is a game of distance and direction. Try to use the club that will get you the right amount of distance if good contact is made.

The pros and low handicappers live and die with distance. It's the first and usually foremost bit of knowledge they want to know, especially when hitting a shot into a green.

○ **Know the course you are going to play**. In competitive golf we play a practice round before the competition, hopefully with the use of a good yardage book (available at most courses).

If there is no book available, we will make our

own, stepping off yardages from specific land-marks into the center of the green. We use sprinkler heads, trees, shrubs, bunkers, or anything else fairly permanent and measure by steps from the center of the fairway adjacent to the mark to the center of the green. We work hard on developing a three-foot step. Older sprinkler systems usually have the sprinkler heads 30 yards apart so we practice walking between those. Most courses have 150-yard markers of one kind or another, usually measured to green center. We always double-check these in a practice round.

It's vital to know distance if you are a competitor, especially around greens where you might have to carry a shot over a bunker in order to reach some pin locations.

○ **If you play one course a lot, try to keep your thinking cap on at all times because it's easy to get careless on occasion.** For example, you walk on the tee of a par-3 hole with a club already in your hand because you usually hit this club on this hole! We all do it. But be alert. This is when the course can whip you!

○ **Make sure all your equipment is in good shape, in place, and ready to go.** Nothing is worse than to reach for something and find it missing. Remember to dress for the weather conditions and be prepared for any changes. When was the last time you forgot a towel; umbrella; tees; rain jacket; sun lotion??

○ **Warm up before playing.** It takes only 20 to 30 shots to get ready to play. Take some shots with every other club in the bag, ending with the driver. See how the ball is moving that day. Go to the putting green to await your tee time. If you have to rush on the tee, the least you should do is take some good stretchy swings with a couple of iron clubs. Be as ready as you can be for that first shot as it just might set the tempo for the whole day!

# 9 Cash In with Straight Drives

Putting is the most important part of golf because of the number of times you must do it during a round. But the tee shot is not far behind putting in priority.

A good tee shot sets you up physically on the fairway to play your second shot with some confidence. And, more importantly, a good tee shot gives you a feeling of elation as you follow it down the fairway.

Notice that I said "tee shot," not "driver." The driver is the club most of us pull out of the bag when we walk on the tees of par 4 or 5 holes. I call this to your attention because, for the most part, the driver could be left in the bag, particularly if you are a high-handicapper. The odds are in your favor if you hit something less than the big one.

A solid 3- or 4-wood will have a better chance of finding the fairway because you will hit it higher and straighter. Of course, you have to decide what kind of shots you want; those that are longer and probably more crooked or those that are shorter but straighter.

As your game and your swing develop, you can work more and more with the driver to get that extra yardage—in play. Try this following game someday when you're on the course and not particularly playing for score:

Use your driver off proper tees. Each time you hit one that goes off the fairway into rough or other trouble, play it for score. But also take one other ball and place it on the fairway approximately 200 yards off the tee, count it as one, play it into the green and also play it for score. See which ball scores the best.

Depending on your abilities, you may wish to use a different yardage off the tee than 200. I set this figure as a respectable drive for an avid player. Take heed from the professionals who play difficult courses and often revert to their 3-wood or a long iron off many tees to give them a better chance to put their ball in play rather than in trouble. I'll bet you will put a better swing on the lesser club also—and just maybe hit it as far as the driver anyway.

Many players ask me if there are situations in which you shouldn't use a tee on the teeing ground. I don't believe so. Teeing the ball is an advantage allowed by the rules. How high you tee the ball can vary, but for starters, tee the ball so that if you placed your driver behind the teed-up ball, half of the ball would sit above the top of the clubface. When using a lofted wood or iron, you want to tee the ball so that it looks like a perfect lie on the fairway—sitting up nicely.

Most players should hit their tee shots away from trouble. If trees line the left side of the fairway, hit from the left side of the tee. On 3-par holes, if the pin is cut to one side of the green, tee it up on the opposite side of the tee. The whole idea is to get a better angle, percentage-wise, to shoot at your target. If the wind is blowing from one side or the other in a cross pattern, tee it up on the side from which the wind is blowing and hopefully gain some wind-aided distance.

Avid players ask me about curving the ball one way or the other and the pros and cons of doing so. I tell them that most players do curve the ball; in fact, it's a lot easier to control if you do bend it a little left or right with consistency.

If you are working with the usual 40-yard fairway and try to hit the ball down the middle, you only have a 20-yard margin for error in each direction. But if you hit down the left side and fade it, then you have 40 yards of fairway to hit.

The straight shot is the hardest one to hit. You can probably hit your short irons pretty straight since the clubs are shorter in length and steeper in loft, making them easier to keep on line. Use your curve smartly off the tee. The good players can curve the ball each way if they have to, though favoring one over the other for most of their shots. Strong players like to fade the ball for carry and control, but many players can hit it a lot further by drawing or hooking the ball because it will run quite a bit further after landing with the hook overspin. It's a choice that each player must make some time in his development.

Do your game some good and the old coach a favor; really give your tee shots some thought as well as practice. In this regard, one of the great players of all time, Henry Cotton, had this to say: "Just before you play, make up your mind never to play a careless shot. Try on every one. Never try to do more than you know you can reasonably achieve. Have a clear picture of what you intend to do when playing each stroke. Play each hole to a plan. Do not strike off the tee aimlessly."

# 10 The Smart Approach

It's really fun to hit that high-arching iron shot into a green and watch it bounce a couple of times and come to rest close enough for a try at the putt—birdie or otherwise! If the pros could give this shot a name, it would be called the "Money Maker" because, in a statistical way, there is a close simile between "Greens Hit in Regulation and Good Scores," and "Making Money"!

What we are looking at here are lots of different places and shots we might have to play in a round of golf, so let's try and analyze some of them. I might ask you at this time if you play USGA Rules (playing the ball as it lies) OR if you move the ball around to improve your lie (Winter or Preferred lies). I often suggest to my beginners to improve their lies in their own fairways because they will have enough problems making contact as it is, without worrying about a tight lie, BUT I try to also encourage everyone to play the ball as it lies. This is the *only* way to learn how to hit the necessary shots and play GOLF! At first you may not score quite as well playing USGA rules, but you will be playing correctly and toward an acceptable handicap. What I have discovered over the years might surprise you! Playing the ball as you find it makes you really concentrate and *this* leads to *better shots* and *lower scores!* Remember, there is always a way to make a shot and that is one of the thrills and certainly one of the challenges of the game. Let's look at some of these shots.

*From the fairway* and hopefully a good lie, our first thought is *distance*—how far do I have to go to the hole? After that I have some determinations to make based on my own swing and game. Envision your own ball sitting there at 150 yards from the pin on one of your favorite holes and think along with me as we both stand behind the shot and try to plan what we should do. What club can I use to hit the ball 140 or 145 yards in the air so as to carry it right into the flag? Or, is the hole so cut that I cannot try to carry it in? Or, am I capable of carrying it in there? Can I land it short and bounce it into the pin? If there is a bunker guarding the green (flag), then I will have to carry it with a nice high shot and probably one more club accompanied by a courageous swing or bail out to a bigger opening to the green further from the hole but in a position that I can either 2-putt or chip it close.

If you are adept with your iron play, remember that the center of most greens is usually no more than 20 to 30 feet from the hole at the worst, and that's not a bad place to be. If you are a decent player, shooting at the pin might give you a challenge and a thrill, but sometimes it is certainly not the smartest thing to do, especially on tough courses. Here you will find the best pin positions guarded by bunkers, high rough grass, slopes, and trees which make it very difficult to get the ball up and down. The middle of the green is a fine target in any case. If your game is such that you cannot hit the ball 150 yards, pick out the best area in front of the green as a target that will set you up for a good try at a chip or pitch and putt. Good players often have to do this very thing when they drive the ball in trouble and have no shot at the green. They will try to get in front of the green safely and then try to get it up and down for par.

Two factors that have a big influence in approach shot decisions are WIND and FIRMNESS OF THE GROUND—soft or hard. These conditions really test your skill and mettle.

Let's look at wind. Most players USE the wind if it is across simply by aiming more left or right and letting the wind help the ball back on target; taking less club downwind and more club into the wind. Many strong players like to "work" the ball against the wind. An example of this would be as follows: the wind is left to right so the shot would be hit at the flag with a draw type shot, using one or two more clubs than normally required from that distance. This ability to "hold" the ball on line is obviously a nice weapon to have in your arsenal. It's always nice to be able to hit the ball lower when playing into or across the wind so as to keep a bad shot from flying away on you. And, it's not that difficult to learn. Try this some windy day when you are at the practice area. Take two or three clubs lower in number than the one you would normally use, choke it down slightly, play the ball only slightly farther back in your stance, use a shorter backswing and a shorter follow-through. Think, low—low!

Wind adds a dimension to the game that really increases the difficulty of shot-making and there is a book to be written about this phase of the game in itself. Your best weapons when the wind blows are good thinking, a lot of patience, and the realization that it will affect everyone playing that day, so just raise your par a few shots and hang in there!

Firmness, or lack of it, in the turf can create dramatic differences in how you might play a shot. When the ground is soft, as after some good rain or early in the morning after the sprinkler system has been working at night (as some of you gals know who play in the early morning leagues), you just know that you can't roll the ball up there; you have to carry it in to where it has to go, and it will stop! The pros love soft green conditions! They can "play darts" by hitting those irons right at the flagstick! Hard ground calls for a different kind of game that demands a lot of judgment and some luck too, because you have to learn to bounce the ball in there. You have to essentially "Keep the ball on the ground"! Airborne shots can be big trouble. This method of play has a unique place in the game of golf! We all witnessed many examples of this by watching shots on the television broadcasts from British Open venues, and in particular, the Old Course at St. Andrews.

Now, with all that discussed, let's put our body to work on this shot. Hopefully, our mind has done its job.

# 11 Out of the Rough and Hills

Did you hit a good shot? I'm sure it was a good decision. Whatever it was, the important thing is that it was your decision and you tried to put a good swing on the shot. Remember to always make your mental decisions before you pick out a club and step into the ball—that's the whole idea!

A smart shot is either one that you know how to make or one that is sure to get you out of trouble. If you play match-play golf, then the gambling shot can sometimes be to your advantage. Personally, I have found that if you play the course and make good shots, you can be an awfully tough match-play opponent.

Let's go back to that 150-yard mark and put you into some different situations other than on the fairway to show how the smart shot can be played. The most common shot for most of us is in rough grass where the ball is visible but the grass interferes when your clubface meets the ball. Remember that! Grass gets between the ball and the clubface. That means moisture. And that means less spin on the ball while in flight, often creating what we all know as a "flyer."

When it does land, it will scoot and run a lot for lack of backspin.

Also, because the longer grass is heavier, it's harder to finish your shot, so it will likely fly lower and bounce more. Often times, in this grass, especially when it is heavy or wet, the hossle gets hung up, turning the toe of the clubface in and resulting in a low-left shot. It's best then to open the clubface slightly when playing from this type of lie.

I heartily advise you to practice these shots when you can because they are most common for most of us and it's kind of comforting to know how to handle them.

One final hint in helping your decision-making for shots out of the rough: simply use a more lofted club for the job. The ball will come out and up a lot easier. If you guess wrong on the lie and the ball doesn't go as far as you thought it might, at least you will be right in front of the green. Experience will make you wiser in these decisions.

Balance is the key when you have a shot from any uneven lie. You must maintain a good center as you swing. You'll know when you err this way because you'll hit it fat or skull it. Take enough practice swings near your ball to determine where the *bottom of your swing* will be. Then set up in that position. This is most critical in uphill and downhill shots. Find the BOTTOM OF YOUR SWING!

Whether we want them or not, we all get stuck with uneven lies over the course of play. It's vital that we know what happens to the ball off these lies and how to reasonably handle them—so here goes:

○ **Uphill**—Keep your weight on the left side and brace yourself solidly inside your right foot to hold balance. The ball will fly higher so use more club. You will pull or even hook your shot, so aim more right of your target. You probably have discovered that the bottom of your swing for this shot is more up off the left heel.

○ **Downhill**—Hold your weight over the right side as you brace solidly inside of the left foot and use an open stance. The bottom of your swing is more toward your right foot. Use less club than usual and aim your shot well to the left of target.

○ **Sidehill, ball above feet**—Hold your weight more toward your toes now and stand fairly tall in address. The bottom of your swing is usually more toward center. This lie dictates pull or hook, so aim more to right of target. Use a club or two longer. You will have to choke down on this shot.

○ **Sidehill, ball below feet**—This is the one where you can fall on your nose if you're not careful to keep your weight back on the heels. Get a good knee flex, squatting down to the ball. This lie encourages an upright swing and a fading or pushed ball flight, so aim to the left in setup and use a club or two longer to compensate for the curve to the right.

As an avid golfer, I'm sure you will agree with me in regard to playing these various shots; it does take some practice, but it takes a larger share of proper technique in order to get the job done. As I state to most of my students, "When you do it RIGHT, it happens!"

# 12 Short Game is Technique plus Feel

Proficiency with shots inside 50 yards is the easiest way to cut strokes off your game. Over 50 percent of your game is played from 50 yards or closer to the flagstick.

These shots are part technique and part feel. And there are many ways to play them. Rather than discuss a lot of method, I'm going to talk about ball flight and roll, and how to get the proper amount of each as required by the shot.

One thought on technique: I see too much wrist activity with these little pitch and chip shots. Control the height of your shot with the clubface and ball position rather than trying to help it into its flight with a lot of right-hand action. Put the club more in the charge of the arms and shoulders.

Your club choice and how much you open the face of the club will determine the height of the shot. Soft hands and a slightly open clubface will deliver a softer, higher shot while firm hands will get you a hotter shot.

Once you discover that swinging the club is the answer to good results, rather than hitting at the ball, then you are on your way to a good short game.

Now, let's analyze flight and roll. First, look at the amount of green you have from the cup to the edge of the green near your ball. This area is your landing strip. Second, how far from the green is your ball located? As you examine these two factors from a good angle, it will give you the big picture as to where you can land the ball and how much landing strip you have for the ball to come to a stop. Once determined, proper shot and club selection can be made.

Here are three shot variations from good lies:

○ **Lot of green to work with and ball close to fringe**—Use a medium-lofted club such as a 6- or 7-iron, square the face, give it a little stroke and let it get on the green and start rolling toward the hole. It's very similar to a putt except you have to get it airborne to land it on the green.

○ **Considerable green to use and your ball is about 15 feet from the edge**—Use a more lofted club such as a wedge or 9-iron to get the ball airborne.

○ **Very little green to work with and your ball about 20 to 30 feet from the edge**—This shot calls for a lot of height so you should use a pitching wedge or sand iron, open the face slightly, hold the club softly, and float one in there.

Any *pitch shot* from 50 yards and in should follow the example of this last illustrated shot. Just tack on a bit more armswing and shoulder-turn and let the lower body kind of follow along. Control the height and firmness of the shot through proper grip pressure and the position of the face of the club.

Practicing these little shots is *fun* as well as vital. I know you are really serious about scoring better, so I encourage you to get where it's at!

# 13 Different Strokes

I wish I could give each of you a guaranteed, surefire way to always get the ball close to the hole with your little pitch and chip shots. I would be richer and you would be happier.

The best I can do, however, besides recommending good technique, is to encourage you to practice.

It takes some doing on your part, but some evening, regardless of the seductions of television, reading, or even cutting the grass, arm yourself with shag bag and clubs, find a friend to go along and head for the nearest practice green. Work on your conventional shots with some of these ideas to guide you:

○ **Choke the club down to the bottom of the grip** (more control).

○ **Play from an open stance** (easier to align to the target).

○ **Try stretching your left thumb down the shaft** (puts the club into left hand more for control of face and path).

○ **Favor the balance of weight on the left side** (easier to get a down-and-through action on stroke).

○ **Keep hands ahead of ball at address and keep them there through stroke** (this keeps club on path and maintains a square clubface).

Here are some other ways to get the ball on and, hopefully, close:

○ **Use the putter.** Some players use it at every turn and I recommend that you give it a try if you're having a problem with this phase of the game. It's harder to control for distance than a lofted club, but once you get the feel for what it's capable of doing, the putter can provide you with a safe way to reach the green and often near the hole without the fear of blading the ball or hitting a fat shot. It's a good play when you are in doubt about a lie or ball position.

○ **Another nifty way to literally guarantee getting the ball on the green from close positions is to use a low-lofted club like a 5- or 6-iron.** Just give the ball a little rap with the right hand in control. Don't worry about follow-through. Just give the ball a little slap. I've seen a lot of good chippers work this way. You can get a bit of spin on the ball and a semblance of control, especially on slower greens. Make the stroke very short and have good acceleration to the blow.

○ **You can use this same slapping or hitting action with your putter, especially from a heavy lie near greenside.** (We refer to this as U.S. Open rough.) Play the ball well back in your stance, even off the right foot. Press your hands well toward the target with your weight over your left side. Pick the putter almost straight up in the back stroke and give the ball a sharp downward blow on the back side, like you're going to beat it into the ground. The ball will jump out of that lie like a scared rabbit and literally run toward the hole with a lot of overspin. You can learn this shot with five minutes practice, and it is especially effective when you have a lot of green to work with.

A good rule to follow when you have a bad lie near the green is similar to the one we use from trouble or a hazard: get the ball out and in play with one shot. It's easy to get cute with some of these shots and play a finesse shot to get close and then just move the ball a few feet where we have to do it all over again. Again, when in doubt—don't! Get the ball on the putting surface where you might have a chance.

Once you develop a knowledge of lies, grip pres-
sures, face positions of club, and different angles of
attack on the ball, you can invent your own shots
around the green, and that's fun, too!

# 14 Bunker Relief

Every golf course has hazards involving water or sand. The only real difference for the player is that water is usually penal, while you can normally make a play of some kind from sand.

In either case, by rule, if your ball lies in either hazard and you try to play it, you cannot sole your club in address or touch the sand/water in your backswing. It's an oft-neglected rule by the avid player and the penalty is severe (general penalty—two shots in stroke play and loss of hole in match play).

Maybe you're one of the many avid players who has a distinct fear of sand bunkers. When one happens to get in your line to the green, do you get a bit anxious about your shot and often times roll it right in there as if it were drawn by a magnet? Bunkers are definitely a distraction. But you can learn to eliminate your fears, just like the pros, who almost relish the sand shot when the alternative is a tough up-and-down from heavy rough grass. Another example for them is illustrated on how many of them play 5-par holes that are reachable in two shots. They aim for the bunkers.

Here are some ways to stay out of bunkers:

○ **On a shot that must clear a bunker and land on the green, think positively about the shot and go through a definite pre-shot routine to get your mind working in that direction.** Remember, the bunker isn't really in your way in a physical sense, it's simply a distraction that you must block out of your mind.

○ **If the shot demands more precise execution than you think you can handle, play your ball to another part of the green instead of to the flagstick or possibly even to the open fringe for an easy chip shot.**

○ **As your shot making and confidence improve with time, you won't even notice that the bunker is there.**

Different ways to get out of bunkers:

○ **Putt the ball.** If there is no lip on the bunker and/or it's quite shallow, you can easily putt the ball onto the green. As a general rule in this situation, stroke the ball about twice as hard as you would from the same distance on the green.

○ **Chip the ball.** From shallow bunkers you can use a lofted club such as an 8, 9, or pitching wedge, and chip the ball out. Be sure to catch the ball first. A little work with this safe shot and you can probably control it quite well.

○ **Explosion shot.** When the bunker is deep and has the usual associated lip at the top, you do not have much of a recourse except to get it airborne and out of there! There are many different techniques that have been developed, but I'm going to give you the adjustments for this shot that I have seen the most over the years. They are as follows:

○ **Use a sand iron.** If you don't have one, I recommend that you get one for your over-all improvement, not just sand.

○ **Work your feet into the sand for stability, balance, and feel.**

○ **Use a narrow and fairly open stance and slightly open clubface.** Put your left hand in control of the club.

○ **Make your point of aim to the left of the target.**

○ **As you start your backswing, cock your wrists immediately so the clubhead is loaded straight up and out instead of the usual back and around as in your regular**

**full swing.** To help you make this move, hold your right elbow closely to your side while doing it. You'll feel it. What this action does is create a steep outside-to-inside path of the club down and through the shot.

○ **The clincher for this shot is to KEEP SWINGING THROUGH THE SHOT!** Get the club to enter the sand behind the ball and don't back off from accelerating through the sand! This is the moment of truth! Don't be a bunker-clunker—keep swinging through the shot.

○ **With the usual practice you will learn how much backswing to take and how hard to swing, plus how much sand to take.**

○ **Practicing these shots is fun, too.** It's a challenge to try different shots, positions, and lies and to figure ways of getting out.

Developing your bunker play will increase your scoring ability and decrease your frustrations and you will have more fun.

# 15 No Fear of Failure

Young people, just learning to play golf, are fun for me to deal with. They are, for the most part, eager to learn, have lots of energy, and have no fear of failure whatsoever. Our golf schools at Michigan State University have given me the opportunity over the years to work with thousands of children which, in turn, has given me the opportunity to study what they want and need the most. The following thoughts are my conclusions on their needs.

○ **Find a mentor—someone to guide you through your stages of growth and development in golf.** Find a teacher who will take time to know you, has your interests at heart, and has a reputation for teaching good mechanics. A good teacher, usually a local professional, will also teach you how to play the game and respect the rules of etiquette and THE game itself. Your original interest in golf was probably instigated by Mom or Dad because they played the game and got you to tag along. They will be a vital part in your learning process together with your "pro."

○ **Get into competition early and play as much as possible.** There are many possibilities available. You will find out in a hurry if you like it or not. Your game attitudes and capabilities will show through, as well as the stark reality of the scorecard. Not everyone is cut out for competitive golf, but those of you who are will discover it and will thrill over the challenge of making a good score or beating a good opponent.

○ **If you are old enough, get into your high school golf program.** You will have good learning experiences and a chance to compete all the way to the state level.

○ **Junior golf programs abound these days and it's possible to fill your summer with competition on a local, state, and even national level.** Check with your mentor to find out at what level you should compete and discuss possible tournaments with your parents.

○ **Practice by yourself.** Find out what you can do with your swing! You must learn to understand your own game as well as the ways of others.

○ **Study the rules of the game—you will be way ahead of the pack.**

○ **Control your temper.** The game is a

continuing test of your personality and character. If you realize this and can accept the discouraging moments as well as the emotional highs, you are accepting the challenge of golf. Try to stay cool and play on a low key for a better chance at success and fun!

○ **Learn to take care of golf courses.**

○ **Always keep up a good pace of play.** Slow play is usually not caused by the lack of skill, but by other factors.

Those are my suggestions to all youngsters in regard to needs. How about what they want? At first they want what we all want—good shots. Airborne shots headed for the target. I get pretty excited when a young player does "it" just right and hits a good one, and I let them know about it. Almost in the same breath, I ask them to do "it" again. The competitors look for good scores and improvement in scoring tactics. The bottom line becomes important and they begin to discover that good swings beget good shots and good shots get good scores, thus they look for help to improve.

# 16 Senior Players Need Motion

It's been said before, "There are things that happen to you when you get older. The first is that you forget everything, the second I can't remember and the third is that you move up to the front tee markers."

If you happen to be in this category and love the game of golf, maybe some of the thoughts that follow will enhance your enjoyment and your skills.

Years ago, as I looked at one of my first classes of senior golfers, I observed one overall deficiency in their swings—a lack of motion. I had to find ways to get things moving so they could hit it a good lick and have a chance to score better.

Here are some recommendations:

○ **Most importantly, find ways to keep your body in playing condition, especially the legs and lungs.** A myriad of methods include walking, riding a bike, stretching, exercise programs, etc. But first, get checked out by your friendly doctor. A proper diet is vital and highly recommended.

○ **Check your grip and make sure that it is soft enough to allow you to cock your wrists properly and release energy through the ball.**

○ **Be sure not to stand flat-footed while swinging the club.** Flex your knees, keep your weight slightly back to the heels, let your weight flow to the right as you swing the club back, and then to the left as you swing the club through the ball.

○ **Try to develop a longer swing and avoid short jabby strokes at the ball.** Try hard to swing the club and suppress hitting at the ball.

○ **Warm up gradually at each outing.** Be prepared to play in any weather. On cool days, dress warmly with layers of loose clothing.

○ **The best recommendation I can make to you is no surprise: practice your short game!**

It would only be par for the course of life if you had some kind of physical ailment, most commonly an arthritic or back problem. All the more important to warm up properly. It's important to utilize your legs a lot, to the extent that you might even sway back and forth some, just to provide some motion and speed to your swing. You may hit some crooked shots this way, but you'll hit the ball a lot harder and have more fun.

○ **Remember, there are a lot of ways to play this game.** An old friend of mine used to step into every shot as in trying to hit a baseball. He was a fine player even though he hit one off the world once in a while. Now that's motion!

○ **Equipment changes could make a dramatic difference in how well you play.** Lighter shafts are here to stay and easier to swing. You might want to try more flexible shafts from what you are using to give you a bit more whip through the hitting area. Check out the different styles of balls and find one that suits your game. The two-piece balls are hotter and are being used by many senior players and they last longer, too.

You may also want to replace some of your long irons with highly lofted woods such as Nos. 5, 6, and 7. They get the ball up in the air quickly with a higher flight, are great for long approaches, hitting from rough grass, and playing long par-3 holes. Most of these clubs are shallow-faced with a lot of weight structure on the sole of the club, both of which encourage good height on the shot.

# 17 Stats Can be Fun and Helpful to your Game

Have you sat down and really assessed your golf game recently? Are you making some strides toward improvement or are you running a treadmill toward a usual "comfort zone?" If you have recorded your scores (many of you belong to a handicap system) you have a "bottom line" figure from which to judge your current position. That is, relative to the courses you play and the people and competition you usually play against. But that's all your average tells you—where you are—not how you got there.

If you like to keep statistics, you may be interested in what follows. Statistics can be a great motivator or just plain fun as you keep track of your performances.

Statistics give you a picture of what you did or didn't do on the golf course. In my business of competitive golf, I use these stats to pinpoint where players need help or what they must spend more time on in practice. We have a special sheet made up upon which we record the following things:

○ **Incidental info**—This is the date, golf course played, the competition played in, and the score on each nine holes.

○ **Fairways hit in regulation**—This reveals your accuracy with your driver and/or other clubs used off the tee. It exposes good or bad thinking off the tee such as, "I should have hit a long iron instead of the driver on No. 3 hole today." Accuracy off the tee has residual effects on other key statistics as well. For example: It's harder to hit greens from the rough than it is from the fairway.

○ **Greens hit in regulation**—Your best in-dicator for scoring, good or bad.

○ **Sandys**—A record of sand-saves. How many successful out and ins out of how many attempts.

○ **Up and downs**—Number of greens missed and number of times you got it up and one-putted. This will tell you if you're saving or losing strokes. This is most important.

○ **Total putts and 3-putt greens**—These two items help you focus on a lot of things, but mainly, "Did I really think each one out and then try and put a good stroke on it?"

○ **Birdies and Eagles**—Celebration time!

○ **Penalty shots**—Just had to bring you back to reality again. Record actual penalties such as out of bounds, lost ball, water hazards, unplayables, etc. Other wasted shots will show up in summary.

○ **Summary**—Analyze and comment on your round that day. Determine where you may have erred but also record where you thought well or had good execution, especially where you needed it.

Stats are not a panacea, but they can be fun and they just might help you improve your play. In golf you always hear these terms: iffa, anda, butta, woulda, coulda, shoulda—as depicted by these comments at the 19th hole: *"Iffa* I had just used an 8-iron instead of a 7 back there on #17 hole, I *woulda* been on the green instead of over and in the lousy pond. I *coulda* made a birdie with an 8 in my hand and at least *shoulda* made par, *butta* I didn't and made a stupid 6 on the hole." Familiar? It's all part of the fun and intrigue in this marvelous game.

# 18 The True Test of Golf

Golf is BIG these days. More and more people are flocking to courses and learning this game with varying degrees of jubilation and frustration. New and beautiful courses are being built rapidly and in great numbers but not fast enough to keep up with the popularity of the sport.

This increased play results in extremely crowded courses. Thus, it reflects the need for a definite awareness of golf etiquette. Rather than list all the things that etiquette entails, let's give it an easy definition and go from there.

Etiquette is no more and no less than taking the time to be kind and friendly to your fellow players or competitors and taking the time to repair any damage to the course that you might create in the normal playing of the game.

If you carry the game beyond the skill level, you find that you can be very successful at golf if you play fairly, by the rules, following the concepts of common courtesy and proper conduct.

I would like to add an important term to our golfing vocabulary —integrity—because many of the game's rules, including the care of the course, depend on self-management. There is no referee out there calling the violations or umpires calling penalties or linesmen telling you to rake bunkers, replace divots, or repair ball marks on the green.

Most of the people with whom I've been associated are good sportspeople and want to play within the rules. However, preoccupation with the play is usually the culprit in regard to violations of rule or attitude. I encourage you to study the rules and learn how to use them. Other players will then follow your example.

Keep your emotions in low gear. If you do this, you will find that you will play better and enjoy it more. Try to be the calm and composed player in your group and see how your attitude diffuses into the others.

The rules of play and etiquette are printed out in the USGA Rule book which is available at most golf shops. If you do not have a copy, I encourage you to find one. Knowledge gained from its use will put you way ahead of the game and make you a much better golf player.

# 19 Improvement Demands Change

The usual request I get from avid players involves correcting ball flight. A most typical request is, "Coach, I'm really slicing the ball. Could you please help me?" My response usually goes like this: "Let's watch your swing and try to determine what causes that slice, then try to correct it. Once we make that determination and I offer solutions, are you willing to make changes and take the time to work them out?"

The key word here is CHANGE. It's a fearful word, especially for the more experienced avid players accustomed to doing things in a certain way. They are coasting in their zone of comfort and are very hesitant, yes, even afraid, to change something. People balk especially at grip changes and minor adjustments in their set-up, both of which by now we know to be most crucial of all. I have only one question for these, in fact, any players, who question change and it goes like this, "You want to improve—now, HOW GOOD DO YOU WANT TO BE?" True improvement comes through changing something by improving technique and then working hard at making the change effective.

If you are willing to believe your mentor or pro and make necessary changes and have the necessary patience, it can be done. It doesn't matter what error you are committing or where the ball goes if you are violating one of the important principles. You must rediscover it through some kind of change and then practice.

Let's review these important principles: AT THE MOMENT OF IMPACT—the path of the clubhead is toward the target, the face of the club is square to the target, the angle of attack is level at the ball, and there should be proper speed to the clubhead.

In dealing with my students, I'll find which of these principles are being neglected or violated and then go ahead with my diagnosis and suggestions for improvement.

Let's continue with the example used in our opening—the slicer! The cause of a slice is an OPEN CLUBFACE. There are different kinds of slices, mostly bad. Let's look at some of them.

> *Ball goes straight and then slices.* If it goes straight to start with, it means your swing path is good but the clubface is open. You have to learn how to square the clubface up at impact by learning a proper release of the wrist lever through the ball.

> *Ball pulled left of target but then slices back.* A lot of people play with this ball flight and

some pretty well so it's not the worst error in the game for sure because the ball usually comes back toward the target from left to right. What you lose with this ball flight is distance. This is an OVER-THE-TOP swing dominated by a quick delivery from the top of the swing and dominated by the shoulders and arms. To correct this ball flight you have to coordinate your timing and use of your lower body to some degree to get your club path moving down the target line. To accompany this timing bit you will also have to work on releasing the club more through the ball. This is a tough change to make because you probably play fairly decently with that pull-slice as it is.

*Ball pushed then sliced.* This flight is caused by picking the club up into the backswing and THEN not releasing through the ball. Major work here and some good drill work necessary. You have to learn how to make a proper armswing away from the ball in your backswing and again, obviously, learn to release the club.

I have always been a proponent of drill work to help people make changes. Drills isolate the error and the correction and give the student good feedback when executed properly. In the case of the slices we have discussed, there are two drills I have found to be the best to help you.

1. FEET TOGETHER DRILL. Hit shots with
a 7-iron, choked down somewhat and using
halfswings with the feet right together. This
encourages good arm and shoulder work and
a proper release of the club in order to *hit the
ball straight.*

2. TRACK DRILL. Using tape, chalk, paint, or
even clubs, make a track toward your target
and about a foot wide. Hit shots from within
the track.   This will encourage a better
backswing and release of the club as you get
feedback from ball flight, divot direction, and
vision of the track itself. Other devices used
for this drill are small boards to get feedback
from sound and feel when you swing on a bad
path and also using a cardboard box on the
outside part of the path to give you instant
FEEL when you swing outside-in.

MOST PROBLEMS can be solved simply by following accepted principles. Here are my general solutions to almost all full swing ills:

O **Find a good grip for you.**  This is the
most important.  The grip controls the clubface. If incorrect for you, the clubface will also
be incorrect and that's trouble.

O **Check your timing.**  The most often violated in-swing fundamental is doing something too quickly.  Usually the answer is to
slow the whole procedure down a bit, but you

should at least try other speeds if you are having a problem.

○ **In pre-swing, check your golf posture and balance so you are ready to swing.**

○ **Check your alignment to the target to see that some part of you is not too open or closed to the target line.** Clubs on the ground can help you here.

○ **Learn to hold your center while swinging.** Feel that you are staying back of each shot. *You cannot hit with either power or control in a consistent manner when you get ahead of the shot.* Most avid players violate this one principle; when you learn to hold through the shot you will realize dramatic change in your performance.

# 20 A Note to the Snowbirds

If you live in snow country and are really nuts over the game as I am, you probably search for ways to "keep your game going." If you do take a couple of months and cool it for the spring, you will come back rejuvenated mentally, but most likely, unprepared physically. Some people like it that way and that's OK! Just so long as they keep on playing and keep on enjoying! It's an important time to me from a personal standpoint and also professionally; I have to keep a golf team in playing condition for late winter-early spring competition.

Here are some things that you can do during the cold months:

○ **Buy an indoor hitting net and place it in your garage or basement.**

○ **Collect or buy used golf balls to hit away into the snow when you feel the urge!**

○ **Find places where you can hit balls during the thaw periods.**

○  **Chip and putt in the house.**

○  **Find an indoor driving range (bubble) in your area.**  Hopefully there will be one within a short driving distance.

○  **Play as late into the year as possible as long as the courses are open and will let you do it.**  In some cold areas you can play right up to the Christmas season.  Keep your feet warm and get the handwarmers heated up! Wear a lot of loose clothing and let 'er go! The late fall is a most beautiful time to walk a golf course.  This also helps to shorten the winter which for us golfers is way too draggy as it is.

○  **Travel south as much as you can afford and play golf.**  Many avid players find ways to do this, as we do.  You don't always have to travel to Florida or other sunbelt states to find courses open.

○  **If you are fairly well confined to "solitary" for the winter, try to at least: a) keep your legs in shape and b) find ways to keep your swing muscles in shape and hit as many golf balls as possible.**

Your legs are vital for a lot of reasons.  If you pack your bag, it gets pretty heavy in the early spring when the courses are still soggy.  If you're a rider, you still need a good set of pins to get the most out of your golf swing!

Your legs are vital to playing golf because they support your posture, provide balance and promote the transportation of weight from one side of the body to the other. I encourage you, depending on your health status, to get into a walking or running program this winter. Good exercise programs might include stretching, rope-jumping, jumping jacks, and toe-raises. Weight training can be good for you for added strength. Before you get involved with an effort such as this, you might want to get professional advice. I would suggest that it's better not to get into it unless you do it right.

You might be interested in (and might want to include in your own activities) some of the things we do in our training program at Michigan State University. We do a lot of the above, but also work on developmental techniques and training methods that might strengthen the swing. We have a large room carpeted with artificial turf from which we can hit shots. We have hitting nets, a simulated bunker, putting gadgets all over the room, mirrors on the wall, a meeting area, and a library. We have TV, VCR, and camera for close dissection of the swing and the viewing of commercial videos. We give our players an opportunity to learn more about golf, the golf swing, and their own swing and game.

Winter is a good time to make change. One can concentrate on technique and performance and not worry about results. Winter is also a good time to study the game and increase one's knowledge of this amazing sport. Good books abound, and there are many fine videos on the market. Reading and watching are neat ways to spend a winter's evening.

Get out your tassle cap, winter boots, and hand-warmers. Find some winter balls (red—of course) and join the snowbird brigade.

# 21 Fossumology 101

How about a course review, so to speak—

○ **Each time you play, try to enjoy the swing you have that day, the people you are playing with, and the beauty of the golf course.**

○ **Always play by the rules of golf.**

○ **Determination can overcome many swing ills.**

○ **More play—less handicap; less play—more handicap.**

○ **Have your equipment checked to be sure you are playing with the right stuff.**

○ **The more you hit, the better you git!**

○ **We all get anxious in this game. Take your time and be cool.**

○ **Study the rules. You'll feel on top of**

things and play better.

○ Play smart and hit shots you know how to hit.

○ Practice from 50 yards and in; that's where it's at.

○ Give each shot your best effort.

○ A contest lasts 18 holes. Never, never give up.

○ Think the shot out before you pull a club out of the bag.

○ If you hit into bad trouble, get out with one shot.

○ You must change *something* to get better.

○ Good luck happens when preparation meets opportunity.

○ Good players have good grips.

○ Fulfill your backswing, especially with your long clubs.

○ Try this to music: "You ain't got a thing unless you got that swing."

○ Always try to swing your arms and the club rather than hit at the ball.

○ You have a chance if you can learn to hold the club and set up in a fairly correct manner.

○ Keep your legs in good shape. They don't hit the ball, but they do get you around and provide the transportation for your swing.

○ Practice hard at holding center and staying behind each shot.

○ You don't have to hit a driver off the tee. An iron could be the right and best choice.

○ Lag the long putts and the very difficult short ones; you might get lucky.

○ If you want to improve, seek out a good teacher and prepare to make some changes.

○ Become better acquainted with the courses you play most often. You'll be surprised at how your scores will improve.

○ When in doubt—don't!

○ Learn to two-putt!

# Order Form

Please send me_____copy(ies) of **Golf made easier—not easy** at $7.95 each.  $7.95 x _____books = _____

Shipping instructions:
I'm adding $1.50 for the first copy and 50¢ for each additional copy_____ (Allow three weeks for delivery.)

Please rush the book to me.   Instead of $1.50, I'm sending $3.00 per book for First Class Priority Mail _____

Total amount of check is_____
           (Please make check payable to Golfish, Inc.)

Name        _____

Address     _____

            _____

Send a copy of **Golf made easier—not easy** as a gift from me to:

Name        _____

Address     _____

            _____

**Golfish, Inc.**
P.O. Box 545
Okemos, MI 48805